MAKING ARROWS

THE OLD WAY!!

by
DOUGLAS SPOTTED EAGLE

Eagle's View Publishing Edition

EAGLE'S VIEW PUBLISHING COMPANY
6756 North Fork Road
Liberty, UT 84310

ISBN 978-0-943604-22-0

10   9   8   7   6   5   4   3

Foreward

Making Arrows the Old Way is the culmination of many years of arrow smithing and study. I have in my personal collection several original shafts and points in addition to access to many museum and private collections, and, with Lyn Wallentine, have been identifying, restoring and replicating Native American Plains Indian artifacts for many years.

Some readers may look at the materials and tools used in the techniques described in this book on arrow making and scoff at the *Old Way* in the title, but I have tried to make it readable for both the experienced and unexperienced craftspersons. For that reason, in most cases an alternative for the use of modern tools is either noted or clearly evident. It is up to the individual reader to decide which technique will work best for them; what is presented herein are not rules, simply guidelines. There are too many rules in our society at present, so don't worry about doing something different than what is presented in this book. Explore the craft. You can indeed turn out beautiful works of art if you simply free your mind of the modern way of doing things and the "old way" is actually easier in many cases. For example, modern cedar shafts have a gloss to them that destroys the authentic look of an arrow while natural rose, dogwood or plum all have the color, spine and composition required for the task.

Last, but not least, there are those who deserve recognition and thanks for their support in this small project. Alton "Longbow" Safford, who is old enough to have lived the old ways and learned from them, and T.M. Hamilton, the author of *Native American Bows* have both spent countless hours with me in the study and craft of arrowsmithing. Carey Beckstead has provided the inspiration for this project. Jim and Virginia Glendenning have helped me to create this book and make it available. Lyn Wallentine deserves much of the credit for this book in its present form. She has seen it grow larger and larger and then smaller and smaller as we underwent the painful process of editing. She was most patient and supportive in this small effort . . .

Although I am solely responsible for the contents of this books, for advice and corrections included in the Eagle's View Edition, I would like to sincerely thank Denise Knight. The number of hours that she devoted to making this a better book are very much appreciated. Also, my thanks to Ralph L. (Smitty) Smith for the graphics work in this edition, to Brenda Martin for proofing the new edition, and to my publisher and editor, Monte Smith.

Lastly, thanks go to the reader who buys this book and who will hopefully help to keep alive the vanishing tradition of making arrows.

Making Arrows the Old Way

Ishi once said, "Any old stick him do for bow, but arrows kill deer." Arrows are works of art and arrows are important.

There are two ways to make arrows: First is the white man method which is to split a round log into squares and then whittle the wood back into round shapes again. Second is the Indian way which is finding straight natural shafts. Either way, the objective is the same. We want a shaft that is straight, free of knots and strong. I have never tried the contemporary method as it seems slow, is less than perfect without machines and lacks the spirit of tradition, so we will forego any discussion of this method.

The Indian way is to choose straight shoots of first growth

Wild Shafts Found Next to a Mountain Road

1

Close-up of Natural Shafts

wood. Wild rose, willow, dogwood, wild plum, witch hazel, river reed, choke cherry, tamarack, currant and wild cherry are all good woods for arrow shafts. Some are better than others, but all will work. Chestnut trees that have blown over usually generate second growth shoots. These have no knots and are straight and strong.

Although the wood you choose will depend on the part of the country you live in, I have listed enough types to give anyone two or three choices. Keep an eye out for shaft materials during your travels. The shaft that killed my first buffalo was cut from a stand of wild rose found in the middle of an amusement park. Make sure and look along river bottoms, on heavily wooded mountain sides and in dark clearings. Once you become conscious of it, you will find shaft material all over the place. A burned out vacant lot recently yielded 200 to 300 shafts.

Personally, I prefer to use wild rose shoots: they are almost perfectly straight, very dense, taper slowly and have great *spine* (they are "stiffer" than a different wood of an equal diameter). An arrow with too much spine will shoot to the left; conversely, an arrow with too little spine will shoot to the right.

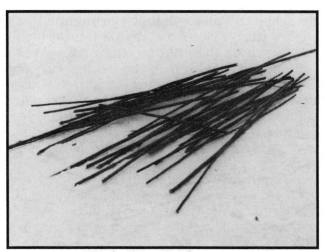

Cut Shafts Ready for Bundling

The amount of spine needed depends on the draw weight of the bow. With a bit of work, practice and experience you can develop small arrows that will shoot with more power from your short bow than is possible from a larger bow with unmatched arrows.

Once you have found shafts to use, cut them. Cut as many as you can, but do not totally deplete the area of growth as it is a good idea to leave some to grow next year. I try to bring

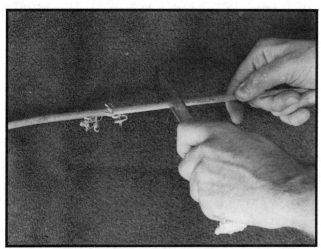

Scraping Off Bark to Prepare for Straightening

3

home fifty to sixty shafts each time I go out and this will yield approximately thirty-five arrows. While it is best to cut shafts from November through April, you may cut them in the spring and hot months. Those cut in the winter will contain less moisture and are less apt to crack or split. If you cut shafts in the summer, do not dry them in the sun; keep them in the shade and turn them each morning as this will help dry them straight. It also works well to bundle twelve or eighteen shafts with lots of string or rubber bands and hang them in your garage to dry.

Once the shafts are dry, you will need to strip or scrape off the bark. If you use willow or witch hazel, you may strip off the bark prior to drying the shaft. A sharp piece of obsidian or a knife blade works well for scraping the shaft as you want to clean down to white wood.

The next step is to cut the shafts down to size. The traditional method requires that you hold the shaft horizontally and place one end against your sternum or breast bone with the other end in your outstretched fingertips. The shaft should be cut where it reaches the end of your fingertips.

Some archers suggest that the Indian method was to measure from the elbow to the end of the index finger plus one finger's length. This is a correct method but will only work if you have used the Indian way to determine bow size. My reach is twenty-five inches, but the average seems to be twenty-seven to twenty-eight inches. There is one exception to this rule of measurement: If you have a short bow, **be sure that the arrow length is no more than half the length of the bow!** For example, a forty-eight inch bow would draw up to a twenty-four inch arrow. Correct arrow length may not even be half the length of the bow, so know when the bow is *stacking up* or near fatal stress. Remember, a full drawn bow is seven-

Shaft Wrench with Groover

4

eighths broken. Never over-draw a primitive bow.

Next, the shafts need to be sorted according to spine, which is done by bending them. Hold the shafts by the ends and, press with your thumbs in the middle of the shaft to bend them. Group them in piles of shafts that bend the same way. Then, take a bunch of those that have been sorted and check them for straightness. If all went well during the drying stage, this should be easy. If not, you will need to use an arrow wrench, like the one illustrated, or you will need to straighten them with heat. I suggest both methods in tandem.

Now identify the butt (large) end of the shaft. This is where the *nock* is cut with the smaller end taking an arrow head at a later stage. The cut of the nock will depend on the release you utilize. If you use the Mediterranean release (most common), you will have to cut deep nocks and bind them to prevent splitting. If you prefer using a pinch or secondary draw, the nock is flared and cut with a small file leaving only a small notch. Some of the arrows exhibited in museums have an "X" nock.

True Plains and Western arrows have enlarged nocks. This is necessary if you are shooting a true pinch (*primary*) or assisted pinch (*secondary* or *tertiary*) release. Enlarged nocks also help recess the binding on the *fletching* (or feathers) and

Nock Bound to Prevent Sliptting

Plains Flared Nock

"X" Style Nock

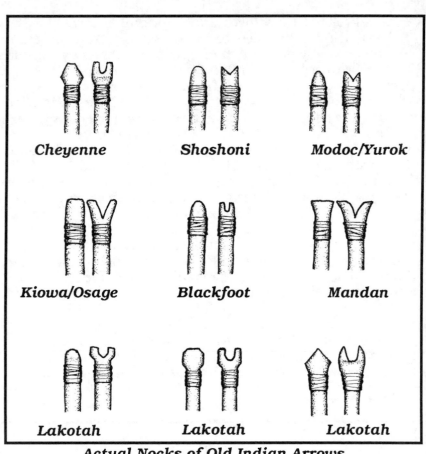

Actual Nocks of Old Indian Arrows

Cheyenne

Shoshoni

Modoc/Yurok

Kiowa/Osage

Blackfoot

Mandan

Lakotah

Lakotah

Lakotah

improve the balance of the arrow. Decide on the type of nock and cut it. You may wish to slightly burn the nock to further harden the wood.

If you are making Indian-style arrows, you need to score or burn *lightning* grooves down the length of the shaft. These have been called "blood grooves," but do not serve this purpose. I believe these grooves help to keep the arrow straight and they may make good *spirit*.

It is time for the easy work. Get feathers, lots of feathers, and sort them into piles of *lefts* (those that turn to the left) and *rights*. Feathers from any bird will work and primary feathers are the best. My personal preference is to use goose, duck or wild turkey feathers. Remember when gathering feathers that the eagle, hawk, owl, falcon and other raptors are protected by

Lefts   **Rights**

federal law.

Useable feathers are like a good shaft, they must be strong and stiff. Tail feathers are usually not stiff enough and this is important as the fletching takes a good deal of abuse both in the quiver and going across the hand.

Now for the part that requires skill. Choose a feather from the two piles (lefts and rights) and place the large end in a vise. Hold the feather by the other end (top) firmly. Grasp the outer side of the feather with your free hand and slowly pull out,

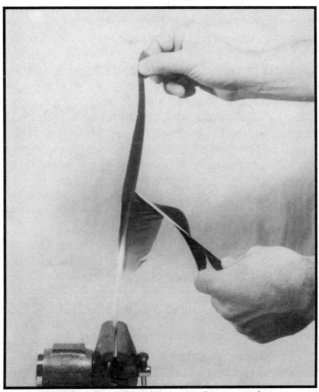

Stripping Feather Using a Vise

down and back with constant pressure and speed. This is called *stripping*. If the vane hangs up at any point, then move your grip further down the vane. If the vane sticks and you continue to pull without moving your grip, you will tear the vane. This method will yield two vanes per feather if you are careful. Never place two vanes from the same feather on a shaft as it will not fly right. The same goes for putting a right and a left feather on the same shaft; the arrow will try to fly left and right at the same time.

Incidentally, there is an alternative to stripping. You can split a feather using a razor blade and then sand or grind the pitch off the vane but the vane will not lay as close to the shaft and stripped vanes last much longer. Practice stripping on old junky feathers. A good hint to more successful stripping is to steam the feathers straight before attempting to strip them.

Sort the stripped feathers according to length, width and height. Place them in groups of three. Cut the groups of three to equal length but do not worry about height until later. Cut small tails in each end of the vane; these will be used for lashing the vanes to the shaft.

A number of different materials can be used to lash down the vanes. Sinew (either real or artificial), dental floss, or waxed linen all work well. If artificial sinew or waxed linen is used, then it will need to be split.

Put your vanes in water to soak overnight as this makes them easier to work with, and they will lie closer to the shaft. Now place one end of the shaft under one arm while holding the nock end in the same hand and place the vane on the shaft and lash one turn around the shaft and over the tail of the vane. Make sure that you place the first fletching on the shaft at a right angle to the nock or the arrow will not leave the bow properly. Now lash the other two vanes equidistant from each other and from the first vane.

Some craftspersons like to trim the vanes at this point. I do not. It seems that once the vane is stable, glued and tied, the cut is easier to make and will be more consistent. Decide for yourself which technique works best.

The Indian arrows I have worked with all have straight fletchings. Most of the fletchings are quite long being five to seven inches in length. You may wish to add a touch of spiral or helix to the vanes as this helps to stabilize the arrow faster after it comes off the bow. It also makes the arrow fly a bit more smoothly. If you do spiral the vane, the side of that feather that

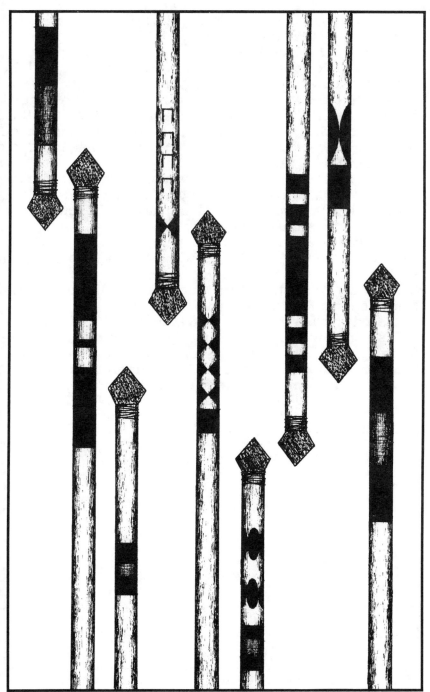

Arrow Crests Found on Indian Arrows

would have faced downward on the bird is the side that should face into the wind on the shaft.

Once you have decided how you want the feathers to lie, you need to tie down the other end of the fletching. Pull the first vane down and lash it tight. Some arrow makers (including the author) like to glue down the entire feather length before lashing down the front. Hide glue is best for this, but barge cement will work just fine. Now glue and/or tie down the other two vanes in the same manner. Make sure you cover the ends of the front tails.

Now glue the lashing at the front and back of the fletching. If you use real sinew on the vanes, rub hide glue over the lashing. Use any type of clear glue on artificial sinew or linen lashing as hide glue will not work with artificial lashings.

There is an alternative to this method of attaching vanes. Indians of South America, as well as some of the North American Natives, lashed on the vanes in reverse and then folded them over so that there is no lashing at the nock point. Many contend that this is easier.

Based on what they have seen in museums and reference books, some arrow makers do not glue the entire length of the fletching to the shaft. What they fail to take into account, however, is that these arrows are over a hundred years old and that the glues on them were not impervious to heat or moisture. Most of these arrows were found on battlefields or

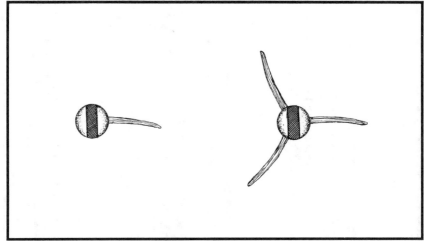

Placing the First Vane at   *All Vanes are Placed*
a Right Angle to Nock   *Equidistant*

in private collections which too often do not receive proper care. This is why the fletchings are very rarely found still properly glued; most museum curators will explain this with a higher degree of articulation than is written here. This is another good point to research on your own.

Since your feathers were wet when placed on the shaft, you will need to steam them over (not in) a pot of boiling water. Simply hold them over the steam for a short period of time and they'll go back to their natural state. Once the vane is back to normal, it needs to be trimmed. Most vanes on Indian arrows measure from 1/32" to 1/8" in height in the front and from 1/4" to 1/2" at the back. To begin, trim them a bit high as you can always cut them down. If the vanes are too high, they will whistle in flight and will not fly far. You do not have to worry about them being too low. Historical research shows fletchings were quite high until around 1650. About that time, someone realized the function of the fletching is to keep the back of the shaft from passing the front of the shaft, and that it doesn't take much of a feather to act as a good rudder. Considering the bow arrived on the Plains only some 2000 years ago, this is quite an evolution. Arrows were originally fletched tangentially (the entire feather was tied to the shaft in a flat form) instead of the radial fletching used today. This shows the keen engineering the Indian developed in a relatively short period of time. At present, fletch your arrows with a long, thin feather and they will be historically correct as well as faster in flight.

Once the vane is trimmed, the arrow is nearly complete and should be tested. Get your bow and some hay bales; soft

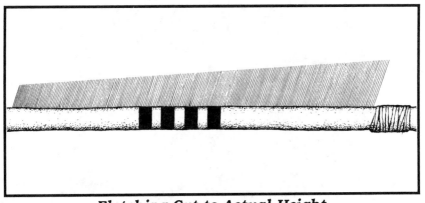

Fletching Cut to Actual Height

Seventeen Steps to Making an Arrow

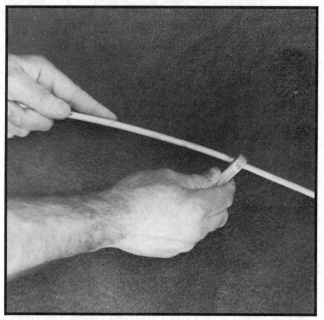

#1 - Straighten the Arrow Shaft

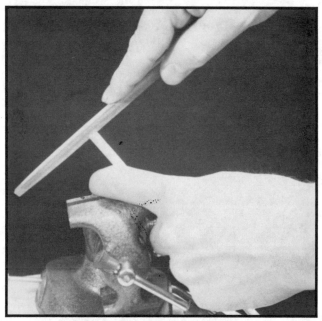

#2 - File the Arrow Nock

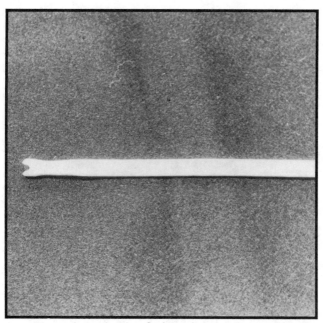

#3 - Completed Shaft (Notice Enlarged Nock)

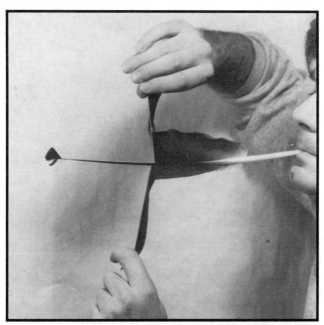

#4 - Strip the Feather in Your Teeth
(Both Sides Are Stripped at Once)

#5 -- Vanes Ready to be Placed on the Shaft

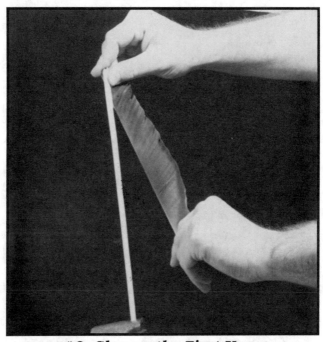

#6- Glue on the First Vane

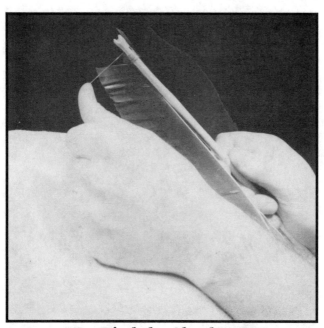

#7 -- *Bind the Glued Vanes*

#8- *Glue Vane Along the Entire Length*

#9 - Pull Up to Let Glue Get Tacky

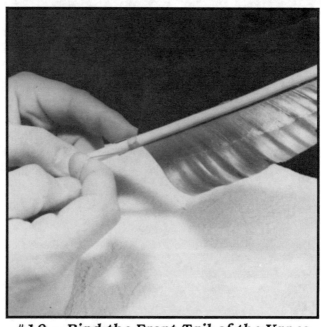

#10 -- Bind the Front Tail of the Vanes

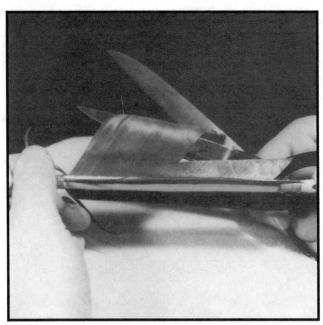

#11 -- Cut the Vane to Size

#12- Tools for Pounding the Arrow Head

#13 -- Arrow Head Made from Pounded Nail

#14- Saw Slot for the Arrow Head

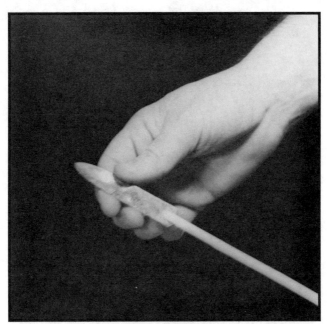

#15 -- Fit the Arrow Head to the Shaft

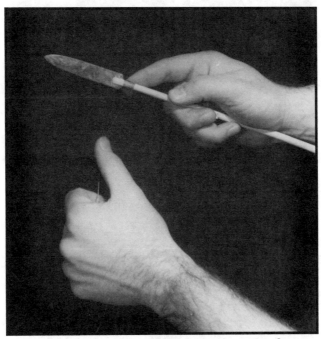

#16- Bind the Head to the Shaft

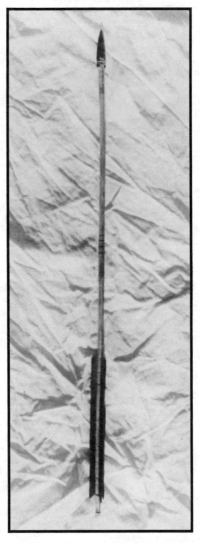

#17 - Completed Arrow

dirt or a sand hill will also work. Shoot the arrows repeatedly
and find those few arrows that shoot better than the others.
Mark them well with paint or marks of some kind. Store these
arrows standing up, not in a quiver and grease them every year
or so and they will always shoot well. They may be used for

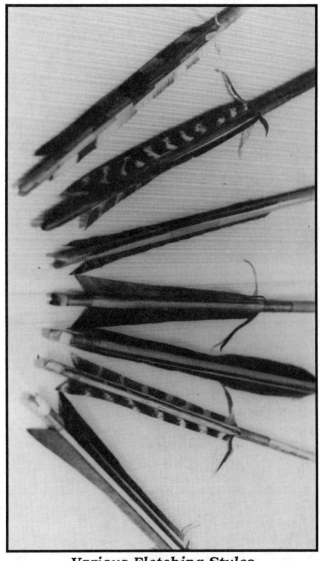

Various Fletching Styles
(Note the Length and Height of the Fletching)

hunting, competition or simply to impress your friends.

✤ ✤ ✤

Many historians have proclaimed that the placement of the arrowhead was determined by whether the arrow was to be used for war or for hunting. If the arrowhead was horizontal to the ground when released from the bow, they reason that, as a man's ribs are in a horizontal position, the arrow was made for war. Using the same logic, if the head was vertical the arrow was meant for hunting animals as their ribs run in that direction. After examining hundreds of arrows in private collections and museums, I doubt very much that this is true. Arrow makers both old and new are well aware that even the straightest of fletchings will not keep an arrow from spinning as it leaves the bow, making head placement a moot point.

Generally, there are five materials which are used to make arrowheads: Bone, antler, stone, wood and steel. If you have access to, or can make, some stone points, you are that much ahead. Stone is good for hunting (though illegal in most states), but will not work for target shooting. The art of knapping, however, is a subject to be delved into on another day.

Wood is only useable when you have the means to make an end that is rounded or blunt. I have seen wooden marbles

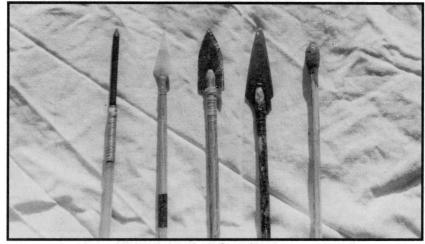

**Arrowheads Made of Nail, Bone, Stone,
Steel and Wood Blunt**

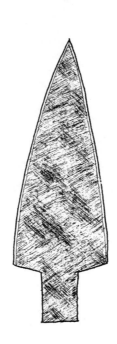

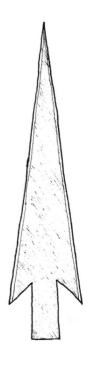

French Trade
Blade
1780-1830

Plains Blade
Forged from
Wagon Rim
Very Common on
the Plains

St. Louis
Trade Blade

**Blade Cut from
Barrel Hoop
Very Common on
the Plains**

**Small Caliber
Shell Used for
Bird or Field
Blunt**

**Southern Plains
Blade from a
Pounded Nail**

**Head Cut from a
Buffalo Leg Bone**

**Natural Wood
Bird Blunt**

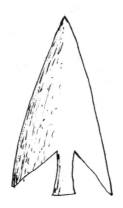
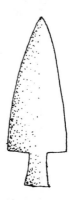

| *Stone Arrow Head* | *Iron Hunting Blade* | *Deer Antler Blade* |

glued to a shaft and this makes an excellent arrow for small game and birds. A clean hit with a wood blunt is preferable, especially on a skunk, to a bad hit with steel. At times you can find wood with a natural mutation that makes a good blunt. Wild rose is great for this. By the way, leave the vanes on a bird arrow a bit longer than those on target or flight arrows. If, by some rare chance, you miss the shot, the arrow won't go as far with higher vanes.

Bone is great for hunting but, like stone, cannot be used for target practice. Using a hacksaw and a file, you can make razor sharp points on bone. This material also looks good and is very authentic. Another natural material that provides a workable alternative is antler. Antler can be shot into bales of hay for target practice, but an antler won't take the edge that bone will.

Last, but not least, is metal. Barrel hoops, old horseshoe nails pounded flat, files, etc. all make great metal heads. Some of the banding steels used today are made of a carbide that holds a great edge. If you can locate an old-time blacksmith, he can fashion heads out of almost anything but be wary of metals with a lot of shine. Bright metal arrowheads look cheap and can possibly scare away game.

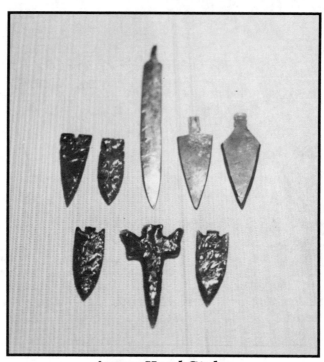

Arrow Head Styles

Remember all of those Hollywood movies where the Indians shot flaming arrows into wagons? Most of that is Hollywood, but Indians did occasionally burn wagons and, as a by-product, think of all of the knives, lances and arrowheads they could make from the wagon rims and tongue hitches!

When the arrowheads are complete, they need to be placed on the shaft. Using a hacksaw or scroll saw, cut a straight slot in the shaft. Place the head in the shaft and see how it fits. If you are using stone or bone heads, you may have to cut a larger slot than is needed for steel. Once you have a good firm fit, take the head out of the slot and sand the end of the shaft at an angle so that the shaft tapers into a smooth extension of the head. Place the head back into the slot and glue it in place with hide glue, pine pitch, epoxy or barge cement. Let this dry for awhile and then lash the head to the shaft with the same material used for the fletching. Once this is accomplished, let the arrow dry in an upright position. As soon as it is dry, and if you have been patient and careful, you should

26

be proud of your new arrow. Make some for your friends and - happy shooting!

FOOTNOTE

Wooden Leg reported that there were many differences between the arrows of different tribes. He described them as follows: The Crow butt end is whittled down to a sharp ridge and the notch is cut across this ridge; the Cheyenne use the same technique. The Cheyenne arrows, however, are tapered to a thin end at the head from a heavy butt end. The Crow shaft is about the same except that the shaft is always fat and heavy. The Cheyenne shaft is slender.

The Sioux arrow has a nock cut extremely flat and the sides

of the nock are beveled to create a sharp ridge on each side of the nock. The neck below the nock is small and tapered up to the neck of the arrow. The wood then tapers back to a thin end at the head.

The Pawnee have a flat butt end with the nock the same as the Sioux. The neck below the nock tapers the same as the Crow and Cheyenne. The Pawnee arrow differs from the Cheyenne in that the Cheyenne arrow has a sharp ridge at the nock and the Pawnee arrow has a flat butt. Further, the Cheyenne arrow has painted lines down the shaft. One old Cheyenne said that all of the old arrows were painted blue in order to remind them of their old lake in the Black Hills.

These differences are noted here to remind the reader that he would do well to consult museum collections and historical accounts if he is concerned with creating arrows that are authentic.